Zoey's Heart

To Ma and Dada for always reading to me.
NOW LET'S READ THIS ONE!

By Zoey Jones
with Wendy Martin

Illustrated by volunteer artists from Pixar Animation Studios

Hearts have a big job.
 They beat. They pump blood.
  They give life!

Before I was born,
 the doctors noticed that I had just half a heart,
  and the half I had was not well.

My name is Zoey. This is my story.

My entire life I've been on a journey
to discover what would make my heart better;
what would make my heart happy;
and what would make my heart whole.

In the wee hours on a Wednesday morning,
  I came into the world
    a little earlier than expected.

The doctors said that all 5 lbs. 1 oz. of me had something called CHD.
                Ma didn't know exactly what that meant,

but I was pretty sure.

Right after I was born, the doctors decided that I needed open heart surgery. I was so tiny that the doctors used tape instead of stitches to close up my chest.

When they were done, I looked like a big present!

(it was my birthday, after all)

For a while, I was so small they had to dress me in doll clothes.

I looked beeeyoootiful!

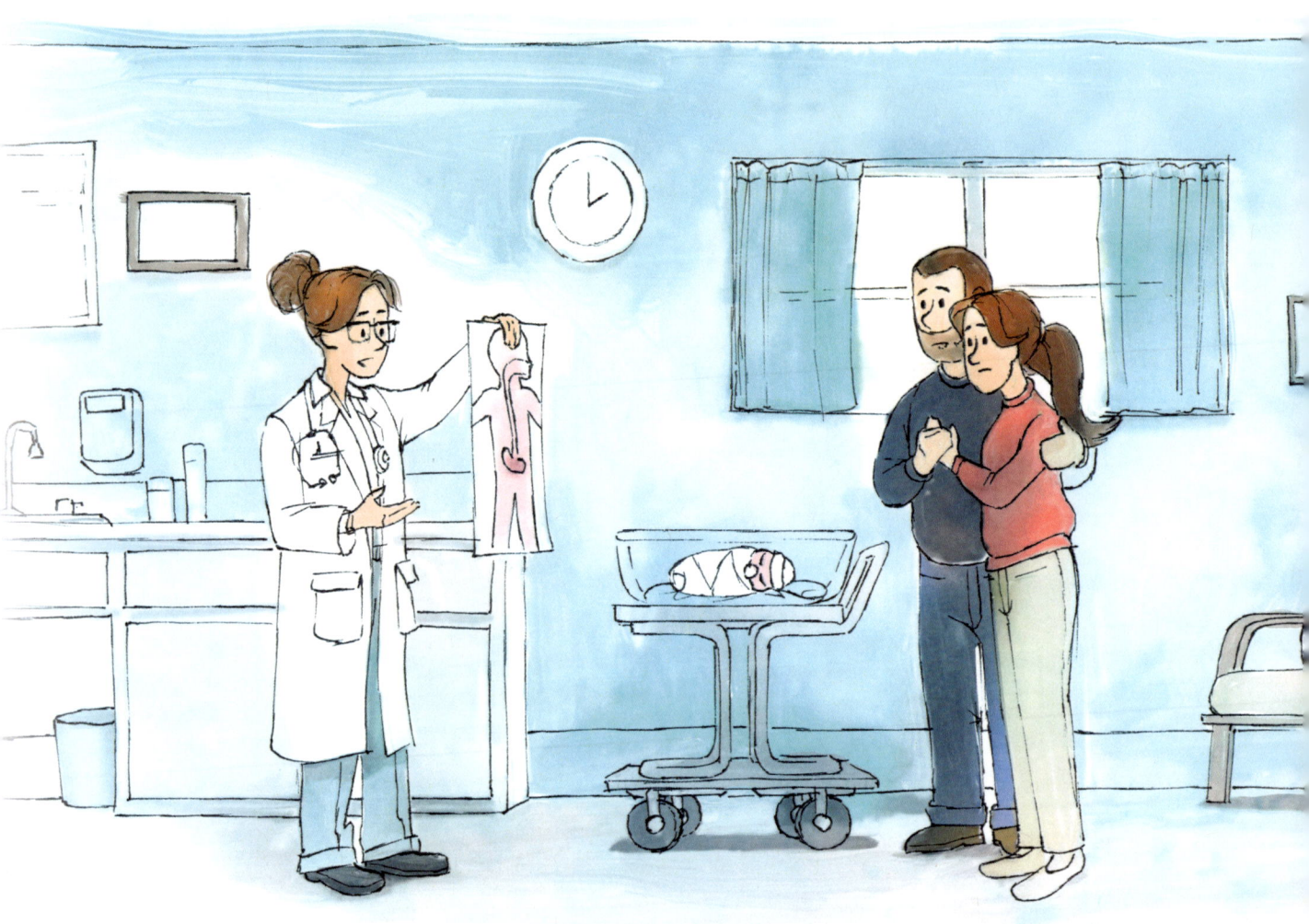

Eating was kind of difficult because my esophagus wasn't connected to my stomach quite right.

The doctors said I needed something called a g-tube.

It was like my belly had its very own super straw!

I also had to be hooked up to these machines - all the time!

But they knew who was boss!

Then things got bad.
    My heart and lungs were so weak,
        the doctors said something had to be done.

We packed up our house
    got on a special airplane, and flew to another hospital.
        They said I'd probably need to be there six whole months!
            I wondered, "Would this make my heart whole?"

it had to!

When we got to the hospital,
the doctors looked carefully inside my chest – and got an idea.
 If they could give my lungs more room to breath,
 I might be okay.

And it worked!
 I could breathe.
  I got to go home!
   Except...

I still had this.
Half a heart.

One good thing about our hearts is they always know us best.
And mine reminded me that my name, Zoey, means LIFE!

And reminded me it would need the very best REST.

(I am sitting down!)

And the right amount of EXERCISE!

and to never forget...

that their hearts were always with me!

And if I DO have a bad day (because we all do sometimes)
I would need to trust in the most important discovery of all.

That our hearts aren't born finished.
A heart is born to be made.

And mine is made of courage.

A note from Zoey's Mom

Zoey was born 4 weeks early. I realized the minute she arrived, life would need to be lived on her time schedule. We knew ahead of time she would be born with severe and complex congenital heart defects, but what we didn't know about were all the other issues she had.

After her birth, Zoey was rushed to the NICU (Neonatal Intensive Care Unit) to be evaluated and stabilized. I didn't even get to see or hold her. The doctors discovered that Zoey's esophagus was connected to her windpipe (instead of her tummy), and her stomach wasn't connected to her small intestines (so she wasn't able to eat). After several hours, they were able to get Zoey stable enough for us to go and see her. They sat us down and explained all of her conditions and the low survival rates that accompanied each one. We questioned. We cried. We wondered if our little girl would even survive. But we knew we would need to be strong, for her, and ourselves.

Zoey had her first surgery when she was just 24 hours old. Another came 48 hours later. We spent the next 8 months in the NICU as Zoey underwent 8 other surgeries. We finally got to take Zoey home, but we didn't get to stay away for very long. The next 12 months were spent living in the PCICU (Pediatric Cardiac Intensive Care Unit) with a very sick little girl. The doctors advised us to relieve her pain with medication and to let her pass away.

We reached out to numerous other hospitals, and we found one that would reevaluate her and offered us some new hope. Nationwide Children's Hospital in Columbus, Ohio was able to do a high risk surgery (that they knew might fail), but our only other option was a heart/lung transplant. We decided to do the high risk surgery first and see how it went...and it WORKED!

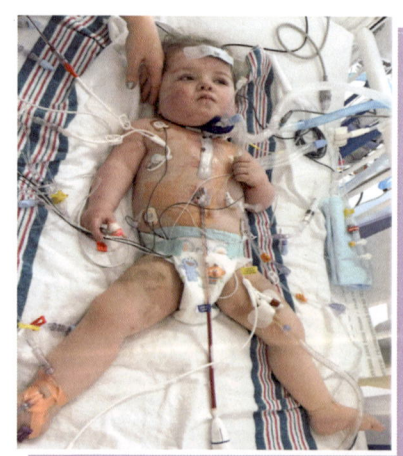

After a 9 hour open heart surgery, Zoey was wheeled out of the operating room, awake, and in great spirits. (Even in her times of pain and struggle, she has always reminded us to stay strong and be

grateful, for every minute.) Her recovery time in the hospital was supposed to take 12-16 weeks, but we were back home in Nashville in 10 days!!!

That was the turning point for Zoey, and things have never been the same. She's been able to stay out of the hospital for longer periods of time. She's become stronger. She even learned to walk (which doctors said would never happen). Years later, Zoey is in kindergarten at her local public school, and is learning what it's like to have some "normal" childhood adventures. She trick-or-treated for

the first time. She went to Disney World and met her favorite princess. She's been able to go to the movies and have play dates with other kids. She's gone to the beach and has felt warm ocean water on her feet.

We weren't sure we would ever get to do these "mundane" childhood activities, and we cherish every single one. Zoey has survived 13 surgeries (3 open heart), 5 strokes, 7 cardiac arrests, and 22 months of inpatient treatment in the hospital. She is truly an extraordinary girl, and her heart is most definitely made of courage.

–Tori Goddard, (Zoey's mom)

About Congenital Heart Disease

Families like Zoey's understand the impact of Congenital Heart Disease (CHD), but most of the public does not.

Here are some facts:

♥ Nearly 1 in 100 newborns are born with CHD

♥ 15% of babies born with CHD won't live to see their 18th birthday

♥ 40,000 infants are born in the US each year with CHD

♥ 25% of babies born with CHD need heart surgery or other interventions to survive

♥ Congenital Heart Disease is the #1 cause of birth defect related deaths

♥ There is no cure for CHD. The disease is lifelong and requires ongoing, specialized care.

♥ Kids with CHD might look healthy on the outside, but they fight for their lives on a daily basis.

♥ Even a small cold can lead to heart failure, even death.

For more information about this disease, visit the Pediatric Congenital Heart Association's website at conqueringchd.org.

If you are a family impacted by this disease, know that YOU ARE NOT ALONE. ♥

Glossary and list of support devices:

ESOPHAGUS – The passage that carries food from the throat to the stomach.

G TUBE – If someone can't swallow food, they need a gastro, or "G" tube. The G-tube is connected to the belly so the stomach can be fed directly.

VENTILATOR – Sometimes called a "breathing machine". This device pushes air into the lungs, and lets it back out again.

PULSE OXIMETER – Blood has oxygen in it; something every part of the body needs. This small device (that fits on a finger or toe), measures that oxygen to see if the body has enough.

OXYGEN CONCENTRATOR – If the blood doesn't have enough oxygen, an oxygen concentrator helps out by filling the blood with lots of oxygen to keep the body happy.

An important note:
Zoey's body has been growing stronger every day
and doesn't need most of these machines anymore.
By the end of 2019, she will probably only need her G-tube!

Make-A-Wish Middle Tennessee exists to grant wishes to kids facing critical illnesses. The goal is simple—to grant every eligible wish! When a wish kid like Zoey makes a wish that requires expertise, we get to engage our community. There is nothing more powerful nor more inspiring than watching a community connect and work together to make a wish come true.

Beth Torres, President & CEO
Make-A-Wish® Middle Tennessee

Zoey's Heart was produced for Zoey as a collaboration between:

middletennessee.wish.org

A Novel Idea Foundation
Nashville, Tennessee
yaywords.com

and volunteer Artists from Pixar Animation Studios
Mathieu Cassagne, Guillaume Chartier, Ethan Dean,
Stephanie Hamilton, Emilie Goulet, Tony Kaplan, Noah Klocek,
Tanja Krampfert, Tia Kratter, David Luoh, Daniel McCoy,
Laura Meyer, Gini Santos, Terry Song, Benjamin Su,
Paul Topolos, Emily Wilson, Maria Yi, Celine You

Copyright © 2019 by A Novel Idea Foundation
All rights reserved. This book or any portion thereof
may not be reproduced or used in any manner whatsoever
without the express written permission of the publisher except
for the use of brief quotations in a book review.
ISBN 9-7805785435-6-7
A Novel Idea Foundation
609 S. Riverbend Ct, Nashville, TN 37221
www.YayWords.com

www.ingramcontent.com/pod-product-compliance
Lightning Source LLC
Chambersburg PA
CBRC092338290426
44108CB00008B/140